SEPTEMBER 2016

Militancy and the Arc of Instability

Violent Extremism in the Sahel

PRINCIPAL AUTHORS
Jennifer G. Cooke
Thomas M. Sanderson

CONTRIBUTING AUTHORS
J. Caleb Johnson
Benjamin Hubner

A Report of the
CSIS TRANSNATIONAL THREATS PROJECT and the
CSIS AFRICA PROGRAM

CSIS | CENTER FOR STRATEGIC &
INTERNATIONAL STUDIES

ROWMAN &
LITTLEFIELD

Lanham • Boulder • New York • London

About CSIS

For over 50 years, the Center for Strategic and International Studies (CSIS) has worked to develop solutions to the world's greatest policy challenges. Today, CSIS scholars are providing strategic insights and bipartisan policy solutions to help decisionmakers chart a course toward a better world.

CSIS is a nonprofit organization headquartered in Washington, D.C. The Center's 220 full-time staff and large network of affiliated scholars conduct research and analysis and develop policy initiatives that look into the future and anticipate change.

Founded at the height of the Cold War by David M. Abshire and Admiral Arleigh Burke, CSIS was dedicated to finding ways to sustain American prominence and prosperity as a force for good in the world. Since 1962, CSIS has become one of the world's preeminent international institutions focused on defense and security; regional stability; and transnational challenges ranging from energy and climate to global health and economic integration.

Thomas J. Pritzker was named chairman of the CSIS Board of Trustees in November 2015. Former U.S. deputy secretary of defense John J. Hamre has served as the Center's president and chief executive officer since 2000.

CSIS does not take specific policy positions; accordingly, all views expressed herein should be understood to be solely those of the author(s).

ISBN: 978-1-4422-7968-1 (pb); 978-1-4422-7969-8 (eBook)

Center for Strategic & International Studies
1616 Rhode Island Avenue, NW
Washington, DC 20036
202-887-0200 | www.csis.org

Rowman & Littlefield
4501 Forbes Boulevard
Lanham, MD 20706
301-459-3366 | www.rowman.com

Contents

Acknowledgments

This report would not have been possible without invaluable contributions from a distinguished group of security experts who served as the project's Senior Advisory Group (SAG).

This advisory group provided guidance and substantive input to the research team, and included:

- General Carter F. Ham (USA Ret.), former commander of the U.S. Africa Command

- Ambassador Mark Bellamy, former U.S. ambassador to Kenya

- Arthur Boutellis-Taft, director of peace operations at International Peace Institute

- Hunter Keith, Libya country director for DAI, Inc.

This report benefited from the guidance of the SAG, but the contents within should not be construed to represent the individual opinions of any SAG members.

The authors would also like to thank the U.S. Department of Defense for its generous support of this study.

Further thanks go to CSIS research assistants Jessica DiPaolo and Maria Galperin, as well as the following group of interns, whose tireless efforts and outstanding research contributed substantially to the report: Kathleen Tiley, Malick Ba, Nikita Mann, Hannah Werman, Ngozi Olojede, Justin Gradek, and Hayley Elszasz.

A Note about Sources and Methodology

Obtaining primary source material on the violent extremist organizations discussed in this report remains difficult. Parallel to desktop research, the principal investigators conducted field research abroad in Mali, Niger, Nigeria, and Senegal, during which they interviewed sources from NGOs, current and former government officials, as well as members of various international peacekeeping missions. This report would not have been possible without their cooperation.

01

Introduction: A Fragile Region under Threat

In March 2016, masked gunmen armed with AK-47s and grenades stormed a popular beachfront resort in Côte d'Ivoire leaving 19 Ivoirians and foreigners dead and 33 wounded. Among the victims was a boy shot at point-blank range while kneeling in the sand and pleading for his life. Al Qaeda in the Islamic Maghreb (AQIM) and al Mourabitoun, an AQIM spinoff, claimed responsibility in a statement released in Arabic, French, Spanish, and English.

A few days later in Nigeria, in Ummarari village on the outskirts of the northeastern city of Maiduguri, a young girl slipped into a mosque during morning prayers and detonated explosives hidden under her clothing. A second girl waited outside the mosque, triggering another suicide bomb as worshippers fled and villagers rushed forward to assist. The blasts, coordinated by Boko Haram, left 24 people dead and 18 wounded.

These incidents, and others like them, attest to the enduring lethality of violent extremist organizations in the West African Sahel. They underscore the ability of these groups to adapt their tactics and strategy as the context in which they operate evolves and to use timing and social media to preserve their air of invincibility. Five years ago, these attacks would have been inconceivable. Suicide bombings were unknown in Nigeria prior to 2011, and the enlistment of young girls in such attacks was unthinkable. Similarly, in 2011 few would have predicted that AQIM's reach, previously confined to the southern reaches of the Sahara Desert, would extend to the West African coastline. Today these attacks elicit shock but not surprise.

A Rapid Ascent and Recent Setbacks

Since the early 2000s, violent extremist organizations have expanded their ambitions, capacities, and geographical reach into the Sahel and West Africa, with devastating impact on human security and economic development. Attacks by AQIM and Boko Haram have killed tens of thousands of people and displaced millions more within and across national borders. Boko Haram killed 6,500 civilians in 2014, and 11,000 in 2015—more than were killed by the Islamic State (ISIL) in Syria and Iraq in the same period.[1]

---

[1] Institute for Economics and Peace, *Global Terrorism Index 2015: Measuring and Understanding the Impact of Terrorism* (New York: Institute for Economics and Peace, 2015), 4, http://economicsandpeace.org/wp-content/uploads/2015/11/2015-Global-Terrorism-Index-Report.pdf.

Together, Boko Haram and AQIM have taken a terrible toll on communities that were already fragile and economically marginalized. Terrorism has disrupted health and education services, devastated local economies and infrastructure, and destroyed ancient shrines and manuscripts, a source of enormous reverence and pride for Malians and the region's Sufi Muslim majority.[2] Extremist groups have been able to seize control of strategic towns in Nigeria and Mali and turn significant swaths of territory into no-go zones for regional governments and security forces. In the case of Mali, violent extremists helped precipitate state collapse.

In the last three years, both Boko Haram and AQIM have come under increasing pressure, a result of regional and international military interventions (notably by France) and a UN peacekeeping deployment into northern Mali. Both groups have suffered significant losses in men and materiel, and they no longer control or administer territory in their respective areas. This progress is important and warrants acknowledgement. However, there is a long way to go before the appeal and the threat of violent extremism in the West African Sahel is suppressed.

These organizations survived previous setbacks, and the local dynamics and underlying conditions that allowed them to emerge and thrive are largely intact. The demonstrated mobilizing power of extremist ideologies and the continued profitability of criminal enterprise and competition across the Sahel will provide incentive for these organizations to regroup and will inspire successor groups to emulate them. Commitment and coordination by regional governments and international partners are essential for progress; current efforts need expansion and sustainment.

New Alliances, New Rivalries, and a Toxic Libyan Spillover

Among the most important sources of resilience for Africa's violent extremist groups has been the fluidity of partnerships and rivalries within and among them. The expansion of links among sub-Saharan Africa's major extremist nodes—AQIM in the Sahel and Boko Haram in the Lake Chad Basin[3]—has been a source of considerable concern to security analysts. To varying degrees, these groups have shared training and tactics, drawn inspiration from one another, and provided each other's fighters with fallback positions when needed.

Today, an additional concern is the possibility of new alliances forming as existing extremist groups inspire and make common cause with other leaders and groups that mobilize around grievance and perceived injustice. In Mali, AQIM and its affiliates are finding partners in the country's center and south among Peul/Fulani communities. These traditional herders are part of a much broader West African community that is finding its traditional way of life increasingly challenged by climate change and competition with agrarian communities over access to water and pasture.

---

[2] Ahmad al-Faqi al-Mahdi, a former member of Ansar Din, was brought before the International Criminal Court on charges of ordering the destruction of cultural heritage sited. He pled guilty in August 2016. France 24, "Malian jihadist pleads guilty to Timbuktu shrine destruction in historic trial," August 22, 2016, http://www.france24.com/en/20160822-mali-icc-justice-timbuktu-jihadist-cultural-heritage-destruction.

[3] This study is limited to the central and western areas of Africa's Sahel region, and does not include an examination of the third major group and area of concern, al Shabaab in Somalia and the Horn of Africa.

As worrisome as new alliances among extremist organizations is the possibility of new rivalries within and among regional extremist organizations. These rivalries may drive competing factions and ambitious leaders seek to distinguish themselves with increasingly spectacular assaults across a far wider geographic zone. The November 2015 hotel assault in Bamako, and more recent, similar headline-grabbing attacks in 2016 in Ouagadougou and at a beach resort in Côte d'Ivoire, may be indicative of a new phase of one-upmanship and has put the entire West Africa region on edge.

Looming over this regional context is the possibility of deepening ties between Sahelian groups and international terror organizations. Boko Haram pledged its allegiance to ISIL in 2015, renaming itself Islamic State in West Africa.[4] AQIM has remained an al Qaeda affiliate since 2007. All of these groups are coming under increasing pressure, a development that could spur greater collaboration between international groups and their local affiliates, as well as competition between rival coalitions. Either outcome will be dangerous for the region and beyond.

As ISIL and al Qaeda struggle in their original strongholds in Iraq and Syria, fighters from both groups have found a fallback position in the violent pandemonium that has engulfed Libya since the collapse of the state in 2011. Both groups have sought to draw in recruits from the broader region to gain an edge against each other and against the various militias and rival government forces seeking to assert or protect themselves in the contest for power. The ISIL and al Qaeda split that is playing out in Libya mirrors a much broader global rivalry between the two terrorist networks, which in turn is enmeshed in geopolitical rivalries among Iraq, Iran, Saudi Arabia, and Syria. As ISIL and al Qaeda compete for new recruits and local allies, there is an urgent need to prevent the Sahel from becoming a proxy battleground.

An immediate priority must be to fortify the countries of the region against possible spillover from Libya and the Middle East and prevent Boko Haram and AQIM from regenerating. The more difficult task, however, will be to tackle the political and socioeconomic drivers of criminality and conflict that underpin violent extremism. This will require fundamental changes in how states are governed and how citizens and communities relate to one another. There is little certainty that Sahelian states will take on this challenge.

This report examines the evolution of extremist groups in the Sahel and the complicated interplay of political, social, and economic pressures that have shaped their strategies, and capabilities, and their sources of potential resilience. It examines the response of regional and international governments, the consequential impact of Libya, and looks forward to possible scenarios and priority areas for concerted regional and international action.

---

[4] Previously, Boko Haram members referred to themselves as Jama'atu Ahlus-Sunnah Lidda'Awati Wal Jihad, "Group of the People of Sunnah for Preaching and Jihad." The group is most widely known as Boko Haram, which is most often translated as "Western education is a sin."

02

The Context: Corruption, Fragility, and Hardship in the Sahel and Lake Chad Basin

Media reports and security analyses often describe the upper reaches of the Sahel[5] as "vast ungoverned spaces," evoking images of a no-man's land in which impoverished and helpless communities are overrun by criminal networks and terror organizations. Flying over parts of northern Mali can reinforce this impression: an arid, rugged landscape, few roads and little infrastructure, and few visible signs of habitation. But these depictions obscure the many layers of structural vulnerability, conflict, corruption, and competing interests within the region that contribute to insecurity and that have allowed violent extremist groups to rapidly expand.

The territories in which AQIM and Boko Haram operate are vast, but they are not entirely "ungoverned." Rather, they are governed by a complex and diverse set of political economy and geopolitical forces, socio-ethnic relationships, and trade and trafficking networks that have evolved over decades and, in many cases, over centuries. State authorities are not absent in this interplay of influences, but they often operate outside the formal structures of the state. Efforts to extend the authority and security presence of the state will consequently be ineffective unless there is a fundamental shift in the dynamics of the broader political economy.

To diminish more permanently the appeal of extremism and terrorist tactics, national governments and their international partners will need to mitigate the enduring structural vulnerabilities of the region. At the same time, they will need to disentangle and reconfigure the varied interests and relationships that have allowed violent extremism and other forms of militancy to thrive. Neither task will be easy, but the latter will likely prove the more vexing challenge.

---

[5] The Sahel (which derives from the Arabic word for "shore") is a semi-arid zone that stretches across the African continent from Senegal to Eritrea, dividing the Sahara Desert to the north from the grasslands of the savannah to the south. The term "Sahel" has also come to signify a loosely defined geopolitical zone that includes Mauritania, Mali, Niger, and Chad, and sometimes Senegal, Burkina Faso, and parts of northern Nigeria. Some of these states encompass large stretches of the Sahara within their borders, and some, like Mali, dip into the savannah zone. The focus of this report is the areas in which AQIM and Boko Haram have been most active—Northern Mali, and the Sahelian/Saharan regions of Niger and Chad, which we will call the "Sahel"; and the Lake Chad Basin area, which includes North East Nigeria, the Lac region in western Chad, the Diffa region of southeast Niger, and the northern tip of Cameroon, which we will call the Lake Chad region.

Structural Drivers: Multiple Layers of Vulnerability

The communities of the Sahel face an interrelated set of economic challenges, with chronic stressors, recurrent crises, and mounting pressures for land, resources, and employment making these states among the most vulnerable in the world. Niger, Chad, and Mali have for many years languished at the very bottom of the United Nation's Human Development Index (HDI), which measures basic indicators like health, education, and standard of living. Nigeria and Cameroon have fared somewhat better, but despite considerable national wealth derived from oil production, both have remained in the HDI's "Low Human Development" category.

Nationally aggregated numbers do not capture the full picture of poverty and vulnerability in the communities most at risk. The areas in which violent extremist groups have taken root are among the most disconnected from national political life and basic indicators—child and maternal mortality, level of educational attainment, and empowerment of women—are, with few exceptions, significantly worse than national averages. In many cases, they are the worst in their respective countries.[6]

Environmental degradation and climate change have added a layer of vulnerability to an already fragile economic setting. The vast majority of Sahelian populations are dependent on agriculture, pastoralism, or livestock farming for food and livelihoods, all of which are highly sensitive to climactic change and exogenous shocks.[7] The annual rainfall average across the region has dropped precipitously since the 1970s, and seasonal floodplains and marshes have narrowed and in some cases disappeared. Lake Chad and its associated wetlands have contracted by 95 percent in the last half-century.[8]

---

[6] In Borno State, 69 percent of women and 63 percent of men have never attended school; in Yobe State, 85 percent of women and 83 percent of men have had no formal schooling. Nigeria's national averages for people with no formal education are 38 percent for women and 21 percent for men. See ICF International, "Nigeria 2013 Demographic and Health Survey," June 2014, https://dhsprogram.com/pubs/pdf/FR293/FR293.pdf. Also in Borno, 80 percent of the population never accesses print news, television, or radio. Across the border, in the Lac region of Chad, 98 percent of women and 93 percent of men never access media of any kind. République du Tchad, *Enquête Démographique et de Santé et à Indicateurs Multiples au Tchad (EDS-MICS) 2014-2015* (N'Djaména: Institut National de la Statistique, May 2016), http://dhsprogram.com/pubs/pdf/FR317/FR317.pdf; and ICF International, "Nigeria 2013 Demographic and Health Survey."

[7] In Niger, 84 percent depend on agriculture; in Mali 76 percent, and in Chad, 68 percent. (Nigeria has a more diversified national economy, although agriculture remains the largest source of employment, and particularly so in the country's north.) See Philip Heinrigs, "Security Implications of Climate Change in the Sahel Region: Policy Considerations," Organization for Economic and Development Cooperation, 2010, https://www.oecd.org/swac/publications/47234320.pdf.

[8] UN Environment Programme, "Vital Water Graphics: Lake Chad, almost gone," http://www.unep.org/dewa/vitalwater/article116.html.

A rapidly expanding population compounds all of this. National population growth rates among Sahelian countries range from 2.9 to 3.9 percent annually, and fertility rates are among the highest in the world.[9] Almost half of the population across the Sahel is under the age of 15.[10]

Nigeria, already at 182 million people, will bound past the United States to rank third most populous on the planet with 460 million people by 2050, according to United Nations Development Programme (UNDP) figures.[11]

The upshot of these trends is that a growing number of people are competing for a diminishing stock of fertile land and water. Pastoralists are expanding their range southward in search of adequate grazing and water, encroaching on areas that have traditionally been used by sedentary farmers. Moreover, to meet rising food demands, farmers are expanding their production zones into areas traditionally used by pastoralists.[12]

Traditional livelihoods are becoming less viable over time, and at present, there are few other good options. A predominantly young population faces a future with few employment opportunities. For the region's growing population of young men, this also means that their chances of marriage—and hence the social stature of adulthood—diminish as well. This latter factor alone figures prominently in the appeal of violent extremist group membership.

The Governance Deficit

The future of the Sahel need not be so bleak. Better water and land management strategies, investments in infrastructure, agriculture and marketing support, education, increased access to family planning, and exploration for (and the fair distribution of the proceeds from) mineral and natural gas reserves all could slow or even reverse the current economic decline. To date, these kinds of investments have not been a priority for the region's national leaders, who are most often focused on power dynamics among political elites in the capital than on nationally inclusive development.

Nigeria, Chad, Mali, and Niger have all undergone long periods of military rule, and democratic norms and institutions remain weak. Further, although national elections take place at regular intervals, election outcomes are rarely determined by government performance or service delivery, but rather by patronage and identity politics. Across the region, the gap between leaders and citizens remains vast. As a Nigerien analyst put it, "Our political structures are not producing success. They are not producing goods, and they are not improving the well-being

---

[9] In Mali, the average number of live births per woman is 6.2, and in Niger the average is 7.96, the world's highest. See "Fertility rate," https://www.google.com/publicdata/ explore?ds=d5bncppjof8f9_&met_y=sp_dyn_tfrt_in&idim=country:MLI:USA:NER&hl=en&dl=en.

[10] Gates Institute, "Realizing the Demographic Dividend: The Science in Service to the Sahel," http://www.gatesinstitute.org/sites/default/files/DDSahelStatement_English.pdf.

[11] UN Department of Economic and Social Affairs, "World Population Prospects, the 2015 Revision," https://esa.un.org/unpd/wpp/.

[12] UN Environment Programme, "Livelihood Security: Climate Change, Migration, and Conflict in the Sahel," 2011, http://postconflict.unep.ch/publications/UNEP_Sahel_EN.pdf.

of young populations. Leaders are aware of the divide and the dissatisfaction, and the instability that could result, but their reaction is self-protection, not reform."[13]

Political dynamics have evolved differently within each national context, but among the core commonalities have been the divide between a centralized state and its marginalized peripheries, the weakness of local government institutions, and the corrosive effect of corruption.

Mali

Until its rapid political unraveling in 2012, Mali was lauded in Western development circles as a model of democratic progress and consolidation. But the country's apparent stability and regularly held elections belied growing public resentment of the ruling elite and the enduring weakness of its governing institutions. The Malian public met the military coup that toppled the government just weeks before scheduled national elections with surprising equanimity. Many Western observers underestimated the skepticism with which Malians viewed the elections and the possibility that the process could lead to any real change in governance. "People were fed up with the whole bunch," a Malian businessman explained. "The political class is all the same—corrupt and indifferent."[14]

The concentration of power in Mali's southern region has been a source of enduring grievance and distrust for communities in the north, and although it is not the only axis of division within the country, it has been a particularly strong one. Malian state authorities have had little incentive to invest resources or attention in the north. The country's mining industry, the largest source of export revenues, is located in the southern half of Mali—*Mali utile* ("useful Mali"), as it is sometimes called. The northern region, with just 10 percent of the country's population, holds little interest for national politicians as a source of economic or political returns—while promising complications and requiring an expensive effort to service.

Animus toward political elites in Bamako has festered among nomadic Tuareg populations in the north since the colonial era and has erupted in full-scale rebellion in 1962, 1992, and most recently 2012. Following a peace agreement with Tuareg fighters in the 1990s, the Malian government launched a process of decentralization intended to transfer more resources and authority to newly created regional and local institutions, but the process was never fully implemented. Locally elected officials were often overruled or sidelined by centrally appointed administrators.[15]

Rather than follow through with genuine devolution of power, successive governments in Bamako have sought instead to conserve resources and manage the north by proxy. Government elites have used patronage and local administrative appointments to coopt and maintain allies and have supported local militias to exploit ethnic divisions and help neutralize challengers. Collusion with influential trafficking networks in the north have helped guarantee

---

[13] Interview with security analyst in Dakar, October 4, 2015.
[14] Interview with Malian businessman in Washington, DC, July 26, 2012.
[15] Hal Lippman and Barbara Lewis, "Democratic Decentralization in Mali: A Work in Progress," U.S. Agency for International Development, 1998, http://pdf.usaid.gov/pdf_docs/pnaca905.pdf.

the loyalty of allies, and at the same time provided a rich source of supplemental income to Bamako elites.

Niger

Niger shares many of Mali's challenges, including a similar geography, a north-south divide that predates independence, and a series of armed confrontations between government security forces and Tuareg forces demanding greater autonomy. The country has undergone multiple military coups, and the process of political liberalization has been intermittent at best.

Nonetheless, Niger has weathered the regional upheavals of the last several years relatively well, compared to its western neighbor. Niger analysts and Nigerien scholars point to several potential explanations. First, Niger's Tuareg communities make up approximately 10 percent of the population, compared to Mali's 5 percent, and the incentives for national accommodation are therefore higher.[16] Niger's uranium mines are located in the areas around the northern towns of Airlit and Agadez. Their strategic importance gives the government incentive to find some accommodation with local communities and maintain an integrated northern security presence. Fifteen percent of mining proceeds, for example, go to local municipalities in the producing regions.

As with Mali, Niger underwent a process of decentralization and integration in the mid-1990s.[17] Although implementation of these reforms has been uneven, local government structures are generally regarded as more genuine and functional than those of its Malian neighbor.[18] None of this guarantees Niger's continued stability: There are persistent political tensions in Niger, and the government has used tactics similar to those in Mali, selectively empowering local authorities to suppress potential spoilers.[19] And, while the Agadez region has seen significant improvements in basic development indicators, other regions of Niger lag behind, including the impoverished Diffa region, where Boko Haram has expanded its presence.[20]

Nigeria

Unlike the countries of the Sahel, which have Muslim majorities, the Nigerian North-South divide has the added dimension of being between Muslims, who predominate in the North, and Christians, who predominate in the South. However, the sheer size of the country—at 180 million, the most populous in Africa—defies easy categorization. Where there is conflict, it is as likely driven by ethnicity, regionalism, land or grazing rights, or by supporters of different political godfathers as it is by religion.

---

[16] OECD/Sahel West Africa Club, *An Atlas of the Sahara-Sahel, Geography, Economics, and Security* (Paris: OECD, 2014).

[17] Interview with Nigerien security analyst, Dakar, October 4, 2015

[18] Interview with professor of political science at Universite Abdou Moumouni de Niamey, January 20, 2016

[19] Stephanie Pezard and Michael Shurkin, *Achieving Peace in Northern Mali: Past Agreements, Local Conflicts, and the Prospects for a Durable Settlement* (Santa Monica, CA: RAND, 2015, http://www.rand.org/content/dam/rand/pubs/research_reports/RR800/RR892/RAND_RR892.pdf.

[20] Knoema, "Niger Development Indicator, 2012," https://knoema.com/NEDAT2012/niger-development-indicators-2012?tsId=1008720.

Nigeria has had elected civilian governments since 1999, when 16 years of military rule ended. The country has a federal political system, and development is supposed to be channeled through the 36 states, although the federal government has little say or oversight on how allocated revenues are expended. Corruption is notoriously high at all levels of government, and much of the money allocated for health, education, and roads and infrastructure does not reach its intended recipients. Local government, in particular, is a weak link in a largely dysfunctional system of delivery.

The 15 years leading up to the collapse of the oil price in 2014 saw Nigeria growing exponentially to become the largest economy in Africa, but most of the boom was restricted to urban pockets largely in the South. The states of Nigeria's North East were long-standing opposition strongholds, and Borno State in particular, which became the epicenter of the Boko Haram insurgency, was largely cut out of the patronage system of the ruling People's Democratic Party. The region lacks significant natural resources, is isolated from the dynamic economy to the south, and suffers from drought and the drying up of Lake Chad. Much of the northeast—which for centuries had been a major trading center connecting North Africa, the Nile Valley, and the South down to the coast—was reduced to an impoverished and isolated backwater.

The sense of grievance at relative impoverishment is sharpened by the high levels of corruption and poor governance. "It used to be that if someone from your neighborhood came home with a really nice car, people would come out to admire it and congratulate the owner," said a state official in Maiduguri. "Now, they are more likely to throw stones at it. People are angry, and they assume people with wealth are corrupt."[21]

A Kaleidoscope of Players: Shifting Alliances and Overlapping Agendas

Government authorities are just one set of the many actors seeking to assert their ascendance and protect their sources of enrichment and control. Across the upper Sahel, a toxic cocktail of armed groups—insurgent movements, ethnic militias, criminal gangs, smugglers and traffickers, and, indeed, violent extremists—compete for preeminence. The lines among these various players are not always clear: membership can be fluid and overlapping, and alliances of convenience emerge and fracture depending on interests, personalities, and the broader political context.

Ethnic groupings are rarely monolithic or unified: Tuaregs, for example are riven by clan and class rivalries and by competition among elite lineages for preeminence. The greatest source of commonality across these disparate groups is antipathy and resistance to the formal extension of state control. Violent extremist groups in the Sahel are woven into the broader infrastructure of competition, conflict, and insecurity, and cannot be understood—or addressed—in isolation from it.

---

[21] Interview with senior government official in Borno State, January 11, 2016.

Traders, Smugglers, and Traffickers: The Region's Economic Veins

Driving through Gao's dusty streets, a few homes stand out, with shiny new Land Rovers parked out front and satellite dishes on the roof. "There's no secret about who the drug-traffickers are," says our driver.

Violent extremist groups in the Sahel operate alongside, within, and across an expansive array of transnational criminal networks that in the last 15 years have seen booming revenues. Trans-Saharan trade has long been the economic lifeblood of the upper Sahel. Although population density is sparse, the region is crisscrossed by trading routes that link key towns with smaller hubs and way stations. Many of the same towns that feature on today's trafficking maps—Gao, Timbuktu, Agadez, Ghat—were key nodes in the trade that linked West Africa's major empires with the Maghreb and the Middle East, some as early as the ninth century.

Likewise, the transnational ethnic, social, and commercial relationships that facilitate modern-day trafficking have been shaped and consolidated over many centuries.[22] Borders first imposed by colonial administrators and then held as immutable (although rarely protected) by newly independent national governments have had little impact on these trade flows, and for most communities outside of the national capitals, territorial boundaries are little more than an abstraction.

With the imposition of national borders and the expansion of sea and air transport in legitimate commercial exchange, ancient trade routes across the Sahara and Sahel have become conduits for a flourishing smuggling enterprise. This is a boon to local traders and consumers, as well as to local government authorities colluding in the trade. Cigarettes, mostly manufactured in Asia, move from the West African coastline to markets in Libya, Algeria, and Europe at an estimated value of $1 billion annually.[23]

Fuel and vehicles, heavily subsidized in Algeria, are smuggled to Morocco, Mali, and Niger. Basic household goods, foodstuffs, and even clothing are also smuggled. In Gao, Mali, the vast majority of imported household goods and foodstuffs are brought in from Algeria according to local residents, even more so now that insecurity has cut the town off from southern markets.[24]

---

[22] Wolfram Lacher, "Organized Crime and Conflict in the Sahel-Sahara Region," Carnegie Endowment for International Peace, September 13, 2012, http://carnegieendowment.org/2012/09/13/organized-crime-and-conflict-in-sahel-sahara-region-pub-49360.

[23] Sahel and West Africa Club, "Cigarette Trafficking," SWAC #15, February 2015, https://www.oecd.org/swac/maps/15-cigarette-trafficking.pdf.

[24] CSIS interview with resident in Gao, Mali, October 10, 2015.

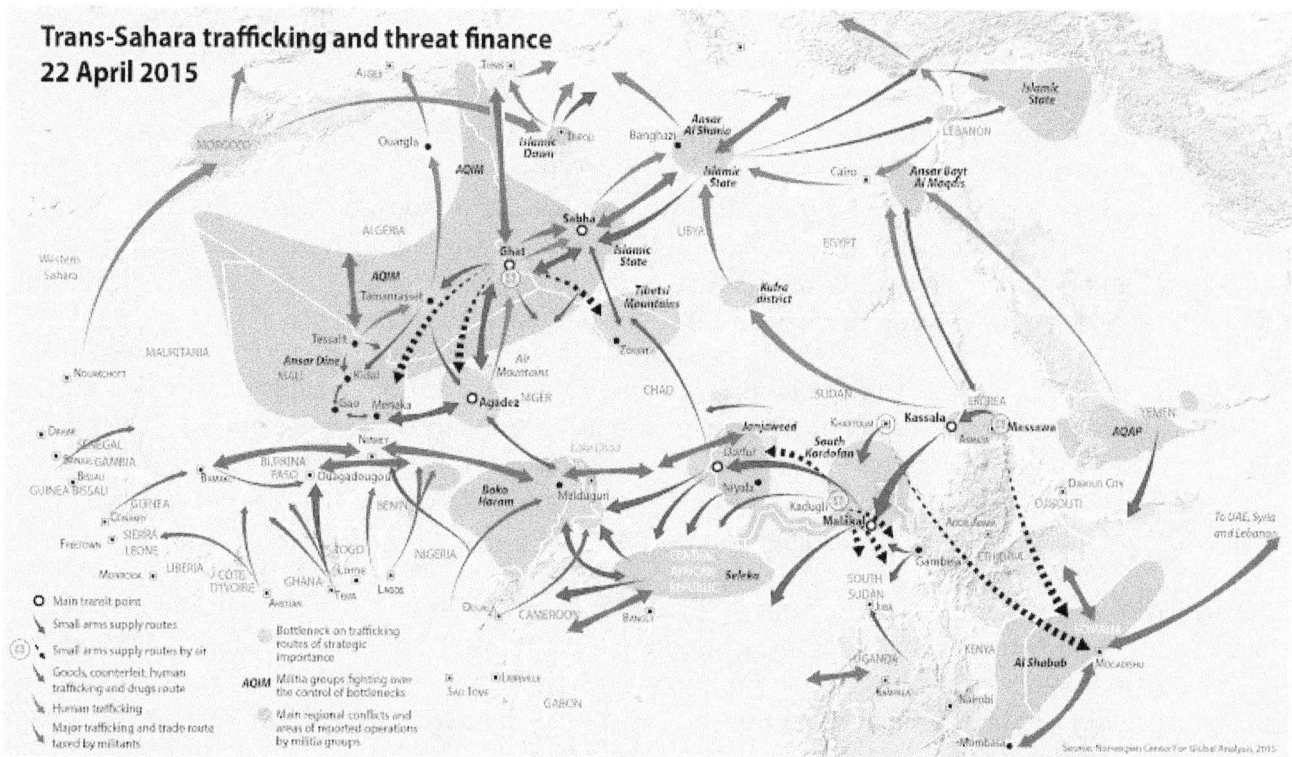

Trans-Sahara trafficking and threat finance 22 April 2015

Source: Global Initiative, "Libya: A Growing Hub for Criminal Economies and Terrorist Financing in the Trans-Sahara," May 11, 2015, http://globalinitiative.net/wp-content/uploads/2015/05/2015-1.pdf.

Trafficking in illicit goods, often commingled with commercial or smuggled cargoes, has expanded dramatically in the last 15 years. Access to new technologies—GPS navigation systems and satellite phones—provides traffickers an edge in caching commodities and evading detection, disruption, and capture. Revenues have ballooned in this brief period, creating a thriving criminal economy.

Narcotics are currently the most lucrative of trafficked goods. As South American cocaine cartels have come under increasing pressure, and access to U.S. markets curtailed, consumers in Europe—and increasingly Asia[25]—have become an important target market. Latin American traffickers have shifted operations and transport networks to the more permissive environment of West Africa and the Sahel, where cocaine trafficking generates an estimated $800 million per annum.[26] While cocaine is the most lucrative among the trafficked narcotics, heroin from Afghanistan and Pakistan, cannabis, methamphetamines, and counterfeit medicine likewise transit through the Sahel.[27]

---

[25] UN Office of Drugs and Crime, *World Drug Report 2016* (New York: United Nations, 2016), xiii, http://www.unodc.org/doc/wdr2016/WORLD_DRUG_REPORT_2016_web.pdf.
[26] UN Radio, "Cocaine Trafficking in West and Central Africa Valued at $800 Million," February 21, 2012, http://www.unmultimedia.org/radio/english/2012/02/cocaine-trafficking-in-west-and-central-africa-valued-at-800-million/.
[27] Ibid.

Trafficking in arms is another source of revenues and insecurity. West Africa and the Sahel are awash in small arms left over from the civil wars of the 1990s, many of them stolen, rented, or sold out of government arsenals by corrupt members of the region's security forces.[28] The looting of Libyan arsenals after the fall of Muammar el-Qaddafi in 2011 reinvigorated a preexisting flow of small arms and light weaponry into the region, including significant quantities of assault rifles, machine guns, rocket-propelled grenades, antiaircraft heavy machineguns mounted on vehicles, ammunition, grenades, and explosives, according to a UN Security Council report.[29] The aftermath saw a surge in the "ant trade" (small shipments of arms that can more easily evade detection than bulk shipments) across the region.[30]

Finally, human trafficking and smuggling have exploded in the last five years, as migrants across sub-Saharan Africa flee insecurity and poverty, and as anarchy in Libya has opened routes, however dangerous, to European coastlines. Thousands are trafficked into sex work, forced labor, or indentured servitude in markets in Asia and the Middle East. Others leave with hopes of finding security and better opportunities in Europe.

The government of Niger estimates that in 2015, between 4,000 and 5,000 migrants per week transited through Niger, with a migrant-smuggling industry that generates profits of $150 million per year.[31] A small but increasing number of Syrians are reportedly seeking access to Europe by flying to Mauritania and attempting the overland route via Gao and Agadez to Libya, Algeria, and Tunisia.[32]

Migrants will often transit through a series of networks—providing transport, safe-houses, falsified documents, sea passage—paying off each segment as they move from one to another. The average cost per migrant is $800, an exorbitant amount for most of those who attempt the trip, and they do not always reach their destination. Migrants who run out of money (or are abandoned) may find themselves stuck at key transit points, unable to move forward or return home. Would-be migrants stuck in trafficking hubs like Gao and Agadez are particularly vulnerable to exploitation, whether through forced or indentured labor, sexual slavery, or impressment into criminal, militant, or extremist groups.

---

[28] UN Office of Drugs and Crime, "Firearms Trafficking in West Africa," n.d., https://www.unodc.org/documents/toc/Reports/TOCTAWestAfrica/West_Africa_TOC_FIREARMS.pdf.

[29] UN Security Council, "Letter dated 23 March 2012 from the Chairman of the Security Council Committee established pursuant to resolution 1970 (2011) concerning Libya addressed to the President of the Security Council," 11, http://www.securitycouncilreport.org/atf/cf/%7B65BFCF9B-6D27-4E9C-8CD3-CF6E4FF96FF9%7D/Libya%20S%202012%20178.pdf.

[30] Ibid.

[31] UN Office of Drugs and Crime, "Launch of the UNODC Regional Strategy against Human Trafficking and Migrant Smuggling," August 25, 2016, https://www.unodc.org/westandcentralafrica/en/unodc-launches-its-regional-strategy-on-tipsom.html.

[32] Katarina Höije, "The Long Way Round: Syrians through the Sahel," IRIN, November 9, 2015, http://newirin.irinnews.org/the-long-way-round/.

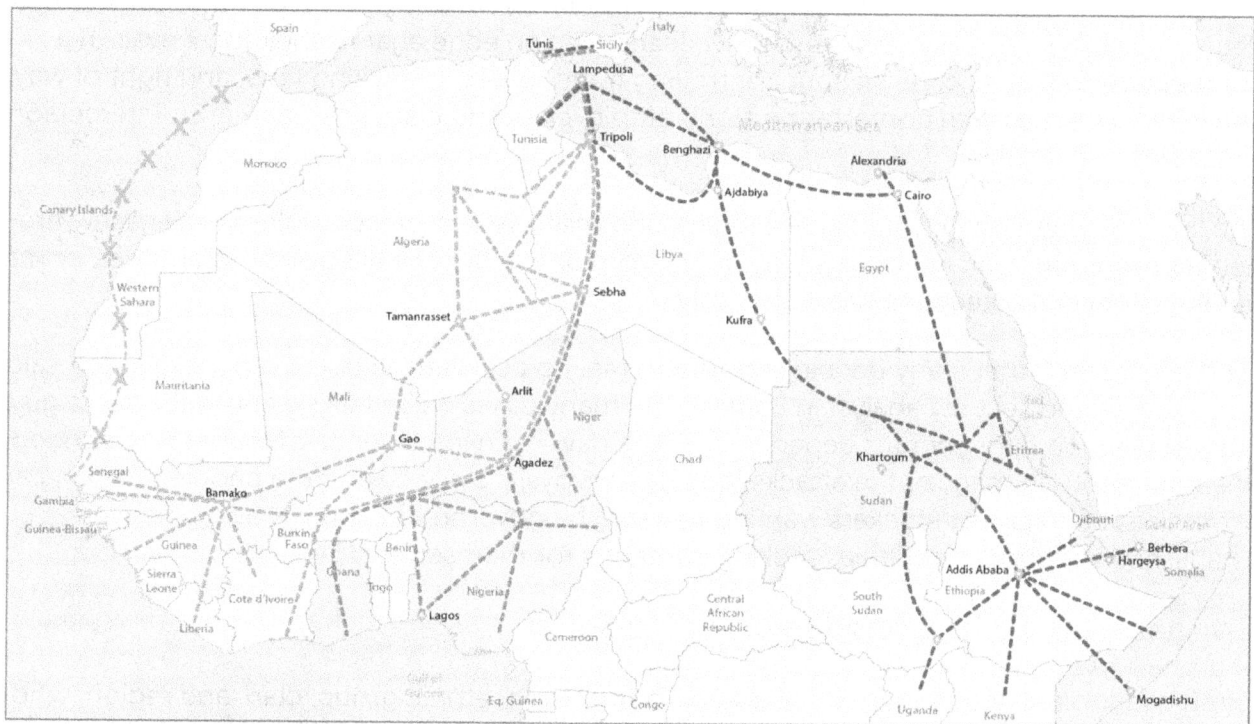

----- Western Route - Main sources countries (shaded): Senegal, Guinea, Mali

----- Central Route - Main sources countries (shaded): Nigeria, Ghana, Niger

----- Eastern Route - Main sources countries (shaded): Somalia, Eritrea, Sudan (Darfur)

--X-- Coastal Route to Spain (closed off)

Source: Global Initiative, May 2014, http://globalinitiative.net/wp-content/uploads/2014/05/3-Routes-Map.jpg.

Rebels, Militias, and Self-Defense Groups

A second set of Sahelian players comprises armed groups that have mobilized around ethnic, clan, and class identities, or around broader national political agendas. While cattle-raiding and herder-farmer conflicts have been a persistent feature of Sahelian life, clashes over land, water, and right of passage have intensified as populations grow and move, and as resources diminish.

Today, the most salient of the politically motivated armed groups are centered in Mali, where factions and coalitions vie for primacy as the government in Bamako presses for compliance with a tenuous peace agreement. Currently, two coalitions of northern groups predominate. First is the Coordination of Movements of Azawad (CMA) or "the Coordination," which is considered "antigovernment" and is largely made up of former separatists who now press for greater northern autonomy within a federal national system. Second is the Platform of Algiers ("the Platform"), a loose coalition of ostensibly pro-government militias seeking decentralization within a unified national system.

While both of these coalitions put forward different visions for a national political architecture, it is not clear that either of these groups wants to see the expansion of formal state institutions into the north. Rather, each coalition sees their preferred model—increased autonomy versus decentralization—as giving their respective leadership an edge against their local rivals in a competition that at its core is about controlling trade routes, trafficking flow, and right of way, and which overlaps with contestation along ethnic, clan, and class lines, and even interpersonal squabbles.

The lines between traders, traffickers, rebels, and militias—and indeed violent extremists—are neither fixed nor clear. Individuals may move from one activity or allegiance to another, or may belong to several categories simultaneously.

"There just aren't that many people in northern Mali to populate all these various groups," said one exasperated security analyst in Bamako. "In many cases we're talking about the same guys, but just wearing different hats depending on the day."[33] An intelligence officer in Gao echoed this sentiment: "in many of the attacks [on UN convoys] it's not clear if the people attacking are extremists, bandits, or traffickers wanting to keep the government and UN away, or even established transport companies seeking contracts for themselves."[34]

Civilians—Last to Be Considered, First to Suffer

Often overlooked are ordinary citizens—civilians of every ethnic group, clan, and region, who have no allegiance to or sympathy for extremist organizations or for the various armed groups that purport to represent them, and who have suffered enormously.[35] Civilians in northern Mali, for example, are keen to see the restoration of government authority, with improved services, a stronger and more accountable security presence, particularly outside the larger towns, and a reinvestment in agriculture and livelihoods.[36] But, their voices and priorities are rarely granted the influence they warrant.

---

[33] Interview with European intelligence analyst in Bamako, October 13, 2015.
[34] Interview with UN security officer in Gao, October 8, 2015.
[35] The NGO Civilians in Conflict has done important work in beginning to document the experiences, voices, and priorities of this often neglected population. See Heather Sonner and Kyle Dietrich, *Fending for Ourselves: The Civilian Impact of Mali's Three-Year Conflict* (Washington, DC: Center for Civilians in Conflict, 2015), http://civiliansinconflict.org/resources/pub/fending-for-ourselves-the-civilian-impact-of-malis-three-year-conflict.
[36] Interview with Tuareg aid worker in GAO, October 12, 2015. Also, see Sonner and Dietrich, *Fending for Ourselves*.

03

The Core Violent Extremist Groups: AQIM and Boko Haram

Violent jihadist movements are not new to the Sahel and the Lake Chad region. Beginning with the rise of West African Islamic empires in the thirteenth and fourteenth centuries, leaders have used the language of Islamism and jihad to expand their sphere of control and subjugate their enemies. Today's aspirants to power have likewise used the language of reform and religious purification to mobilize adherents against corrupt rulers and to subvert established political hierarchies.

Religious fervor has always appealed in times of upheaval and dislocation: in West Africa, Islam spread more quickly with the French colonial conquest than in all the previous centuries. The Sufi orders that emerged during the colonial period provided a source of authority and order and a symbol of resistance, albeit passive, to the occupying forces.

There has been a marked shift toward more conservative expressions of Islam in recent decades, although the vast majority of Muslims across the Sahel coexist peacefully with Christians and other religious minorities. Nonetheless, strong financial support from Saudi Arabia for mosques, schools, and clerics who proclaim a more "pure"—and often intolerant—version of Islam have fed a narrative of division and provided fodder to ambitious individuals seeking to mobilize a following.

Despite their significant differences, both AQIM and Boko Haram have followed this pattern, with charismatic leaders using the language of Islam to capitalize on an entrenched sense of grievance and injustice, to expand their ranks, challenge (or upend) the established order, and build out their zones of influence and protection.

But the language and ideology of violent "jihad" have not been sufficient in and of themselves to sustain the loyalty of these groups' followers over time. Strategies for recruitment include a range of inducements beyond the appeal of a "righteous" cause. Boko Haram early on established a microfinance system to provide small loans and one-off grants to entice members to join. An important incentive for new members has been the promise to finance marriage ceremonies, an expensive undertaking. This is a significant benefit for young men in the region, where marriage, social status, and graduation to adulthood are inseparable elements, and where poverty and unemployment preclude the possibility of marriage and advancement for many.

Groups like the Movement for Unity and Jihad in West Africa (MUJAO), an AQIM offshoot, have appealed to racial, ethnic, and class sentiments, playing to a sense of grievance among segments of the population that rank low in traditional social hierarchies. MUJAO and AQIM made strong appeals to the pragmatic interests of local communities by aligning their Islamist rhetoric with the economic concerns of local communities. In Timbuktu and Gao, for example, AQIM and MJUAO leaders claimed that customs duties, tolls, and tariffs were against the will of Allah and that they would no longer be enforced under Islamist administration.[37]

Even this broad spectrum of inducements has not been wholly effective. While statistical evidence is scant, it is clear that a significant proportion of members joined under threat of death or violence. In Borno State, a Civilian Joint Task Force commander described how a friend of his younger brother was forced to join:

> Boko Haram came to the boy's home in a nearby village. They told him to join them. He said no, and they killed his father. The next day they came back. He said no again, and they killed his mother. The next day they came back and said "we will kill all your family." The boy said, "Okay, I will join."[38]

As Boko Haram's violence has become more gratuitous and disturbing, coercion has become a more important source of new membership. The spiritual devotion that initially drew followers to the group's founder is much rarer today.[39]

Origins and Evolution of Al Qaeda in the Islamic Maghreb (AQIM)

AQIM is arguably the product of a thwarted democratic process. The group has its origins in the Algerian civil war, which erupted after the ruling party annulled parliamentary elections that an Islamist party was poised to win in 1992. As the government sought to root out Islamist sympathizers, a group of veterans who had fought alongside the *mujahedeen* in Afghanistan founded the Armed Islamic Group (GIA), which aimed to destabilize the country through attacks on security forces and a series of massacres that killed thousands of civilians. Algeria's "Black Decade" ended in 1998, and although other opposition groups were eventually granted amnesty, members of the GIA broke off to form the Salafist Group for Preaching and Combat (GSPC) and continued to launch attacks against the Algerian regime.

GSPC gained global notoriety with the high-profile kidnapping of 32 European tourists in 2003. The tourists, mostly German citizens, were eventually released in exchange for a reported ransom of 5 million Euros.[40] The episode had two enduring effects: first, it launched what became an extremely lucrative kidnap-for-ransom enterprise for GSPC and its successors; and

---

[37] Francesco Strazzari, "Azawad and the rights of passage: the role of illicit trade in the logic of armed groups formation in northern Mali," Norwegian Peacebuilding Resource Center (NOREF), January 2015, https://www.clingendael.nl/sites/default/files/Strazzari_NOREF_Clingendael_Mali_Azawad_Dec2014.pdf.

[38] Interview with member of Civilian Joint Task Force, January 11, 2016.

[39] Interviews with Maiduguri residents and CJTF members, January 12, 2016.

[40] The ransom was reportedly paid by the Malian government, in exchange for an equivalent boost in development assistance from the German government. See Kate Connolly, "Germany accused of buying hostages' release," *The Telegraph*, August 20, 2003, http://www.telegraph.co.uk/news/worldnews/africaandindianocean/mali/1439340/Germany-accused-of-buying-hostages-release.html. Iyad Ag Ghali, a former Tuareg rebel commander, who went on to head the Islamist group Ansar Din, was a key intermediary in ransom negotiations.

second, it spurred a more forceful campaign by the Algerian government to expel the group from Algerian soil.

Under pressure from the Algerian military (and, it is alleged, with financial inducements by members of the Algerian intelligence services[41]), GSPC was pushed further into the northern expanses of Mali, Niger, and Mauritania. On the defensive, GSPC's new "emir" Abu Musab Abdel Wadoud, also known as Abdelmalek Droukdel, began in the early 2000s to cultivate a relationship with al Qaeda in Iraq. In January 2007, al Qaeda leader Ayman al Zawahiri announced a union between the two groups.

The affiliation with al Qaeda boosted AQIM's global profile and expanded its regional focus from Algeria to the broader Sahara-Sahel region. Volunteers from Mali, Mauritania, Nigeria, and Senegal joined the group, which organized a network of safe houses, weapons caches, and training camps to prepare fighters from the region. Some of these fighters went on to join conflicts in Iraq.[42] At the same time, AQIM's criminal activities—particularly kidnap for ransom, with demands often up to $10 million per hostage—made it one of the wealthiest of al Qaeda affiliates, with ransom payments alone estimated at $125 million between 2008 and 2014, the majority paid by European governments.[43]

AQIM also generated revenues from narcotics trafficking, forging loose alliances with trafficking networks, and then either taxing goods in transit or charging protection fees. Mokhtar Belmokhtar, a veteran of the Afghan-Soviet conflict and a founder of GSPC, acquired a level of autonomy within AQIM by establishing an elaborate and lucrative smuggling network along the group's southern flank that moved cigarettes, cars, fuel, and arms. Although its leadership has remained primarily Algerian, AQIM gradually and patiently embedded itself within the surrounding communities through payoffs to traditional authorities, partnerships, and marriage. Belmokhtar, for example, is said to have married four women from different local clans.

AQIM, like its antecedent organizations, has lacked cohesion since its inception, as individual leaders have clashed over strategy, tactics, ideological focus, and lines of responsibility. Its splinter groups have been motivated by ethnic, class, and commercial rivalries as well. The MUJAO established itself in 2011 with Mauritanian and Malian leadership, with members drawn to some extent from a broader pool of Songhai, Peul (Fulani), and local Arab communities.

Although still aligned with AQIM—and still led primarily by Arab or "white Moor" commanders—MUJAO's establishment was seen by many as a rebuke of AQIM's Algerian bias and the perceived chauvinism of its leaders toward "black" Africans in its ranks. This may have been

---

[41] Jeremy H. Keenan, "Algerian State Terrorism and Atrocities in Mali," Open Democracy, September 25, 2012, https://www.opendemocracy.net/jeremy-h-keenan/algerian-state-terrorism-and-atrocities-in-northern-mali.

[42] Michael Sheuer, "Al-Qaeda and Algeria's GSPC: Part of a Much Bigger Picture," Terrorism Focus 4 issue 8 (April 5, 2008), http://www.jamestown.org/regions/latinamerica/single/?tx_ttnews%5Bpointer%5D=7&tx_ttnews%5Btt_news%5D=4058&tx_ttnews%5BbackPid%5D=50&cHash=5716c2b8737b0d247f32f0a8ceea37d9#.V74GU00rJpg.

[43] Rukmini Callimachi, "Paying Ransoms, Europe Bankrolls Qaeda Terror," New York Times, July 29, 2014, http://www.nytimes.com/2014/07/30/world/africa/ransoming-citizens-europe-becomes-al-qaedas-patron.html.

more recruitment propaganda than reality, as the vast majority of its membership remains Arabs and Moors from Mauritania, Algeria, and the Western Sahel.[44]

Intra-ethnic rivalries and competition over control of drug-trafficking routes were particularly pronounced in Gao and entwined in MUJAO's creation.[45] Among MUJAO's financiers were wealthy Tilemsi Arab businessmen, two of whom were implicated in the 2009 "Air Cocaine" incident.[46] One of them, according to a Malian intelligence analyst in Bamako, is now a senior leader in the GATIA armed movement, a pro-government militia with a prominent seat in ongoing political negotiations.[47]

Meanwhile, Mokhtar Belmokhtar chafed under the AQIM hierarchy. His growing stature and sense of autonomy rankled other AQIM commanders, who accused him, among other things, of ignoring their calls and failing to file expense reports.[48] In 2012, Belmokhtar split from AQIM to form al-Mulathameen (the Masked Brigade). The 2013 attack targeting the Algerian-based Tigantourine gas facility in In Amenas cemented his relative autonomy and jihadist credentials. Belmokhtar went on to merge his brigade with a faction of MUJAO, creating al-Mourabitoun ("The Sentinels") shortly after the In Amenas attack.

Sahelian extremist groups came into their own with the fall of the Qaddafi regime in 2011. In April 2011, a newly emboldened National Movement for the Liberation of Azawad (MNLA) successfully pushed unmotivated and under-resourced Malian military forces out of northern Mali, seizing the towns of Gao, Timbuktu, and Kidal and declaring the independent state of Azawad. As the Malian government fell to a coup, AQIM, MUJAO, Belmokhtar's Brigade, and Ansar Dine—an extremist group established in 2011 by disgruntled Tuareg commander Iyad ag Ghali[49]—saw an opportunity. Initially making common cause with the MNLA, they quickly took control of the three strategic towns, declaring a northern caliphate and sidelining the secular Tuareg fighters.

After nine months of relative stasis—and as the international community sought to piece the Bamako government back together and muster an African Union peacekeeping mission—Islamist fighters pushed southward, attacking the central Malian town of Konna, just 12 miles from a military garrison in the densely populated town of Mopti. Fearing a further push toward Bamako, French military forces launched airstrikes against the attackers, halting their advance. By the end of January, the French had retaken Gao, Timbuktu, and Kidal. A contingent of West

---

[44] Strazzari, "Azawad and the rights of passage."

[45] Ibid.

[46] Ibid.

[47] Interview with Malian intelligence analyst, Bamako, October 6, 2012. See also Mohamed Ould Mataly, "Il est temps de choisir ton camp," Maliweb, http://www.maliweb.net/contributions/mohamed-ould-mataly-temps-de-choisir-camp-1649472.html.

[48] Rukmini Callimachi, "Rise of al-Qaeda Sahara Terrorist," Associated Press, May 29, 2013, http://bigstory.ap.org/article/ap-exclusive-rise-al-qaida-saharan-terrorist%20%20.

[49] Iyag Ghali, a veteran of previous Tuareg rebellions, had made his fortune in part as a government-sanctioned hostage negotiator in the 2000s. In 2011, he reportedly sought to assume leadership of the MNLA. He was rebuffed and instead went on to form the Islamist Ansar Dine.

African peacekeepers deployed shortly thereafter, transferring authority to the UN Multi-Dimensional Integrated Stabilization Mission in Mali (MINUSMA) in July 2013.

AQIM's southward push proved overly ambitious, and their rapid expulsion highlighted the militants' basic lack of military capacity. The group suffered considerable losses in manpower and equipment and, temporarily at least, in global prestige. Today, however, AQIM and its various offshoots are proving their resilience and adaptability as the agreement among armed political groups unravels and as insecurity deepens.

A Deadly Group Emerges in Nigeria: The Origins and Evolution of Boko Haram[50]

> We thought they were like hippies at first. Our poor uneducated boys who had nothing better to do. Nobody took them seriously. Then we started seeing university graduates tearing up their certificates, engineering degrees, even medical school. And we thought, we need to start paying more attention.—Nigerian journalist in Abuja

Established in 2002, Boko Haram's initial incarnation was as a narrow, insulated sect operating in the remote northeast corner of Nigeria in the Borno State capital of Maiduguri. Its founding leader Muhammed Yussuf called for a rejection of the corrupting influence of Western culture and state authority, and of traditional religious authorities seen as degenerate collaborators in an immoral government system. [51] The group drew its adherents largely from disaffected university students and unemployed youth, many of them members of the Kanuri ethnic group, which has significant populations in Niger, Chad, and North East Nigeria, the regions formerly encompassed by the ancient Islamic kingdom of Kanem-Bornu.

The group expanded its presence in Maiduguri in 2002, militarizing with support from local government authorities. Ali Modu Sheriff, then governor of Borno State, is widely suspected of arming and financing Yussuf's followers in the run-up to the 2003 and 2007 gubernatorial elections as a protection and intimidation force to support his candidacy. Yussuf and Sheriff fell out after the 2007 elections. Sherrif reportedly felt threatened by Yussuf's expanding influence

---

[50] Boko Haram, which loosely translates as "Western education is a sin," is the colloquial name given to the group that originally called itself Jama'atu Ahlis Sunna Lidda'awati wal Jihad (People Committed to the Propagation of the Prophet's Teachings and Jihad). At its inception, the group was also locally known as the Nigerian Taliban. Today, having pledged allegiance to the Islamic State in March 2015, the group calls itself al-Wilāyat al-Islāmiyya Gharb Afrīqiyyah (Islamic State West Africa Province). For simplicity sake this paper will continue to refer to the group as Boko Haram.

[51] Yussuf was an early follower of the Islamic Movement of Nigeria, an Iranian-funded movement led by Ibrahim al-Zakzaky that called for the establishment of Shari'a in northern Nigeria. Many of Zakzaky's erstwhile followers, including Yussuf, eventually left the IMN due to its perceived "Shi'a agenda," a rejection no doubt encouraged by an inflow of Saudi Arabian funding that began in the 1980s and aimed to counter growing Iranian (and Shi'a) influence. Yussuf turned instead to the Sunni "Izala" movement, a Salafist group that called for rejection of the secular Nigerian state, becoming a prominent cleric himself in the process. Yussuf eventually broke from Izala as well, founding Ahl-Sunna wal Jamma (ASWJ, Companions of the Prophet), also then known as the Nigerian Taliban. See Jacob Zenn, "Nigerian al-Qaedaism," Hudson Institute, March 11, 2014, http://www.hudson.org/ research/10172-nigerian-al-qaedaism-.

and reneged on a preelection promise to make him Chief Imam of Maiduguri.[52] The ex-governor has denied the allegations, but they have gained new traction with recent accusations by the current Borno State Attorney General, who has called for his arrest.[53]

After the fallout, Borno State authorities sought to criminalize Boko Haram members by imposing motorbike helmet laws, widely seen as targeting the group, since many of its young members were okada drivers and complained that the helmets would not fit over their turbans.[54] Boko Haram members began to escalate sporadic, low-level attacks—Molotov cocktails thrown from moving motorbikes—against police stations and barracks, and local nightclubs. In July 2009, Nigerian police forces launched a crackdown against the group, killing some 800 members and capturing Yussuf, who was fatally shot while in police custody.

Following Yussuf's death, much of Boko Haram's leadership fled Nigeria across its northern frontiers. Yussuf's top deputy, Abubakar Shekau, who was wounded in the July massacre, reportedly traveled to northern Mali and trained with MUJAO in the Gao region. Other members moved through Chad and Niger to train and fight alongside jihadist elements in Somalia, Algeria, and Afghanistan. They began to return to Nigeria in 2010 and 2011, and Boko Haram reemerged as a far deadlier and sophisticated enterprise. Under new leadership, the group expanded its repertoire of tactics and range of targets, with more and more attacks intended to inflict maximal civilian casualties.

Suicide car bomb attacks on police and UN headquarters in Abuja in June and August 2011, respectively, propelled Boko Haram to international notoriety.[55] As Nigerian forces hardened targets in Abuja, Boko Haram shifted instead to a series of large-scale attacks against civilians in cities in North Central and North East Nigeria.[56]

The government in turn responded and imposed a state of emergency in the three most affected North East states, marked by a brutal and often indiscriminate campaign that swept up many innocents and left villages burnt to rubble as security forces and insurgents engaged in retaliatory attacks.[57] The year-long state of emergency eventually brought a modicum of security to Maiduguri, but Boko Haram shifted to asymmetrical attacks against soft targets, including churches, mosques, schools, and dormitories in rural areas. Boko Haram militants slaughtered students as they slept, and kidnapped thousands of women and girls, including 276 students from the government secondary school in Chibok in April 2014.

Following the Chibok kidnapping, Boko Haram launched a series of attacks across northern Borno State, as well as parts of Yobe and Adamawa. Seizing control of villages and towns, they

---

[52] Interview with Nigerian journalists in Abuja, January 10, 2016.

[53] "Borno Attorney General Says Ex-Gov. Sheriff Created Boko Haram," FreeSpch, August 26, 2016, http://www.freespch.com/2016/08/25/borno-attorney-general-says-ex-gov-sheriff-created-boko-haram/.

[54] Interview with Nigerian journalists in Abuja.

[55] Mamman Nur, Yussuf's third-in-command, is thought to have masterminded the UN bombing, after receiving training and support from both al-Shabaab in Somali and AQIM.

[56] In the first three weeks of January 2012 alone, more than 253 people were killed in 21 separate attacks. See Human Rights Watch, "Nigeria: Boko Haram Widens Terror Campaign," January 23, 2012, https://www.hrw.org/news/2012/01/23/nigeria-boko-haram-widens-terror-campaign.

[57] Dibie Ike Michael, "ICC to Probe Nigeria Army, Boko Haram over Human Rights Abuses," AfricaNews, April 2014, http://www.africanews.com/2016/04/14/icc-to-probe-nigeria-army-boko-haram-over-human-rights-abuses/.

declared a new Islamic Caliphate that at its peak counted 26 local government areas under its control. Capture of these towns owed little to the group's military capacity or strategic acumen; Nigerian military forces, whose rank-and-file had neither the training, equipment, nor leadership to take on this new kind of threat, offered little resistance.

Divisions within Boko Haram's leadership deepened after Yussuf's death. While Shekau remained the public face of the group, there was considerable opposition among its top commanders over his indiscriminate violence against Muslims, growing resentment of his erratic and often violent behavior toward his deputies, and disagreement over the possibility of negotiations with the Nigerian government.

The most prominent split was between Mamman Nur and Khalid al Barnawi, both of whom had developed strong connections to AQIM. Nur established a new group, Ansaru, in 2012, which announced itself as a more "humane" alternative to Boko Haram. Ansaru claimed that it would no longer target Muslims, and would kill Christians and government forces only in "self-defense."[58] "Ansaru orchestrated a major prison break in Abuja in November 2012,[59] and followed this with a series of kidnappings in 2012 and 2013.[60] Nur's offshoot maintained a generally cooperative relationship with Boko Haram, and claimed no further attacks as Boko Haram began taking over local government areas.

In the final year of President Goodluck Jonathan's tenure, the Nigerian government, in partnership with forces from Chad, Niger, and Cameroon, launched a more forceful and concerted military offensive on Boko Haram. That momentum has accelerated under the tenure of President Buhari. Thousands of Boko Haram members and a significant number of its senior leaders have been captured or killed, and thousands more have surrendered.

The group no longer appears to have access to the kinds of equipment and weaponry that it has had in the past. Modes of transport that once included tanks, armored vehicles, and Toyota Hilux trucks have been replaced by Volkswagen Golfs, bicycles, and, in some cases, horses.[61] The Nigerian Air Force has mounted a sustained assault on the group's hideouts in the Sambisa Forest, taking out "high-value" individuals as well as fuel pumps, solar panels, and significant weapons caches.

Many residents of Maiduguri identify the establishment of the Civilian Joint Task Force (CJTF) in 2011–2012 as a critical factor in the fight against Boko Haram. Initially a loosely knit group of volunteers who took up arms—sticks, machetes, and homemade guns—to protect their neighborhoods against Boko Haram, CJTF members became a link between communities and security forces. Most important was their willingness to provide information to the police and military, identifying Boko Haram members, tracing their movements, and turning over suspects

[58] Jacob Zenn, "Leadership Analysis of Boko Haram and Ansaru in Nigeria," Combating Terrorism Center, February 24, 2014, https://www.ctc.usma.edu/posts/leadership-analysis-of-boko-haram-and-ansaru-in-nigeria.
[59] "Prison Break Frees 200 Inmates in Central Nigeria," Reuters, December 7, 2014, http://www.reuters.com/article/us-nigeria-prisonbreak-idUSKBN0JL01320141207.
[60] Connor Gaffey, "What Is Ansaru, the Other Militant Islamist Group in Nigeria Besides Boko Haram?," Newsweek, April 4, 2016, http://www.newsweek.com/what-ansaru-nigerias-other-militant-group-443785.
[61] Interview with Civilian Joint Task Force commanders in Maiduguri, January 12, 2016.

to Nigerian security forces, something that many in the area were understandably reluctant to do.[62]

The CJTF is not without problems. Today there are some 24,000 CJTF members across Borno State. The Borno State government has begun to provide stipends to a small number of trained and vetted members, and some are integrated into the military. But what next for these mobilized, armed, and highly motivated young men, many of whom are jobless? "These boys feel strong and have a lot of responsibility at a young age," said a CJTF sectoral commander in Maiduguri. "If we tell them to go back to whatever they were doing before, they will surely become a nuisance in the future." Others worry that they could very easily be politicized and used as "protection" forces in future electoral campaigns and political debates.

Boko Haram no longer controls local government areas it once did, with a significant number of fighters pushed back to rear bases in the swampy islands of Lake Chad and the forested mountains of northern Cameroon. This is not to say that the North East is fully under effective government control: asymmetrical attacks have continued, targeting camps for internally displaced persons, mosques, and occasionally convoys carrying food. Only days after the CSIS research team visited IDPs at the Dalori camp on the outskirts of Maiduguri, Boko Haram attacked the adjacent village, killing an estimated 85 people while also attempting to raid the IDP camp itself.

The group increasingly uses young girls to perpetrate suicide attacks, in part because they are less likely to raise suspicion, but also, according to a Civilian Joint Task Force commander in Maiduguri, because girls are considered more dispensable as the supply of young fighting men dwindles. In December 2015, President Buhari claimed in a BBC interview that Boko Haram as an organized fighting force was finished, no longer able to launch conventional attacks or engage the military directly. "Technically," he said, "we have won the war." The group is indeed weaker, but it is far too early to declare victory, technical or otherwise.

Current Snapshot

Today, neither AQIM nor Boko Haram hold territory, and both groups have lost considerable weaponry and personnel to national and regional interventions. This has not prevented either group from inflicting considerable human damage, however, and while neither is in a position to engage effectively regional military forces, both have been able to perpetrate asymmetrical attacks and maintain a robust media presence. There is little room for complacency, as both Boko Haram and AQIM have shown an ability to recover from setbacks in the past, reemerging stronger than before.

Boko Haram: Down but Not Out

Boko Haram at present is arguably in a weaker and more vulnerable position than AQIM. The group has lost thousands of fighters and many in its senior leadership, seen thousands of its

---

[62] Jennifer G. Cooke, "Now Comes the Hard Part: Five Priorities in the Continuing Fight against Boko Haram," *CSIS Commentary*, February 5, 2016, https://www.csis.org/analysis/now-comes-hard-part-five-priorities-continuing-fight-against-boko-haram.

captives rescued, and a renewed surge in surrenders to authorities. The Lake Chad region is in the midst of a devastating food security crisis, and as with Boko Haram's millions of displaced victims, many of its own fighters are reportedly starving. "We reported an attack on a village near Maiduguri to the military," said a Civilian Joint Task Force Commander. "The military was able to stop some of them and found their truck piled up with food. They were just skin and bones."[63]

Under sustained assault from Nigerian and regional forces, its leadership has fractured again with a reopening of the rivalry between Abubakar Shekau and Maman Nur. Nur reportedly made another decisive break with Shekau at some point in 2015–2016, taking with him hundreds of followers, including founder Mohammed Yussuf's son Abu Musab al-Barnawi (whose given name is Habib Yussuf).[64]

In August, ISIL leadership announced that al-Barnawi would replace Shekau as leader (or *wali*) of Boko Haram. In an interview with the ISIL publication *al Nabaa*, Barnawi announced that in its new iteration, Boko Haram would reject Shekau's indiscriminate violence and focus more narrowly on Christian proselytizers and churches. Echoing Ansaru's earlier claims, Barnawi pledged that the group would no longer carry out attacks on mosques, markets, and other venues belonging to Muslims. Shekau issued an angry video rebuttal, denying the change in leadership. He has since been gravely wounded, according to the Nigerian military, with some speculating (not for the first time) that he has been killed. CJTF members interviewed in August report violent clashes between the two factions.[65]

Barnawi and Nur are reportedly allied. Their shift in rhetoric and purported targets may indicate an ambition to foment a religious war and to win the support of local communities, which Shekau's indiscriminate tactics failed to do. Whether the new faction will have the capacity to follow through on its ambition is an open question. The leadership split, ISIL's announcement, and the video sparring have put Boko Haram in the headlines once again, but the available evidence strongly suggests that the group remains weakened and under intense pressure, bold rhetoric and propaganda videos notwithstanding.

AQIM, Ansar Dine, Al Mourabitoun: Fractured but Resurgent

AQIM and its affiliates in the Sahel are ultimately more likely to withstand current campaigns against them, having a more agile and fluid network of alliances, and being situated in a political context that appears to be deteriorating. A surge of protests in Gao and Timbuktu, clashes between the pro-government Platform and the separatist Coordination, and continuing attacks attributed variously to bandits, traffickers, extremist groups, and militias, threaten to unravel the fragile peace agreement in Mali. Attempts to establish interim authorities in northern towns are running up against the same vested interests and local rivalries that have blocked the extension of state authority in the past.

---

[63] Interview with CJTF commander in Maiduguri, August 2016.

[64] Hamza Idris, "How Rift Dislodged Shekau in Favour of Boko Haram Founder's Son," *Daily Trust*, August 6, 2016, http://www.dailytrust.com.ng/news/general/how-rift-dislodged-shekau-in-favour-of-boko-haram-founder-s-son/157996.html.

[65] Interview with groups of CJTF commanders in Maiduguri, August 5, 2016.

The deterioration of security is not limited to the northern part of Mali. The contested legitimacy of the state has also driven persistent unrest in central Mali, which has seen rising inter-communal tensions in recent years and an economy hard hit by the prolonged national political crisis. The infrastructure of conflict and insecurity in Mali is thus very much intact, and will likely offer new opportunities for extremist groups.

After a period of relative quiescence in the wake of the French intervention, AQIM, Ansar Dine, and al Mourabitoun reasserted themselves through high-profile attacks on the Radisson Blu Hotel in Bamako in 2015, and in 2016, at both the Splendid Hotel in Ouagadougou, and the L'Étoile du Sud hotel in Grand Bassam. Neither Burkina Faso nor Côte d'Ivoire had experienced this type of extremist violence in recent memory. It is not altogether clear to what extent local networks in these countries helped facilitate the attacks, but the possibility of such coordination has put other West African capitals on high alert.

Also of significant concern has been the rise of extremist allies in central and southern Mali. The Macina Liberation Front (FLM) emerged in 2015 and was founded by Mopti cleric Amadou Koufa, an ethnic Peul who met Ansar Dine founder Iyad Ghaly through the Dawa religious movement. Also linked to Iyad Ghaly is Ansar Dine-South, which emerged in the country's far south, along the border with Côte d'Ivoire. These newer groups may have little inherent capacity, but could signify an expanded network of partners for Ansar Dine and AQIM with the ability to facilitate attack planning and logistics across a wider geographic area.

National, Regional, and International Responses

Although responses to violent extremist groups in the Sahel and Lake Chad Basin have gained momentum in the last two years, they remain hampered by the limitations of national governments and the relatively narrow focus of interventions. Regional governments have been slow—and in some cases ambivalent—to responding. There will be no easy fix for extremism and insecurity in the Sahel and Lake Chad Basin, but at a minimum, it will require a consistent, coordinated, and comprehensive effort by intervening partners.

National Governments

None of the regional governments has the military, intelligence, or law enforcement capacities to mount effective counterterrorism campaigns on their own. None has the ability to control effectively and completely its national territory and all face multiple security and development challenges in addition to the extremist threat. However, capacity issues are only part of the problem.

A first challenge has been ambivalence by national governments to act with urgency and commitment as violent extremist groups gained traction. In Mali, the government was content to leave the north insecure and allowed its security forces to corrode through corruption and favoritism. In Nigeria, the government of President Goodluck Jonathan downplayed the threat posed by Boko Haram, and was reluctant to draw attention to an expanding terrorist insurgency in the North East as he headed into contested elections.

The Chadian government, eager to establish its position as a regional military power, was quick to join with France in the January 2013 intervention into northern Mali, but saw Boko Haram as less of a priority. The government dismissed Boko Haram as a Nigerian problem, despite the presence of rear bases on Chadian soil and arms flows that passed through Chadian supply routes. Chad became active against Boko Haram only when its own strategic transport routes through Cameroon were disrupted, and its armed engagement paid for by Nigeria.

All regional governments have responded almost exclusively with military force, and often with heavy-handed and arbitrary violence. Nigeria's initial response was ham-handed with thousands of young men swept up and incarcerated with little evidence of wrongdoing and no recourse to challenge their imprisonment. Extrajudicial killings and retaliatory attacks against entire villages deepened the sense of distrust and insecurity among local communities.

The last two years have seen a significant improvement in discipline and professionalism of Nigerian forces, who are now better equipped and more confident in confronting Boko Haram. In Niger, 25,000 inhabitants in the Diffa region were ordered in May 2015 to leave the region immediately or be considered supporters of Boko Haram. The government made no provision for transport, food, or shelter, and several died along the way, exhausted and hungry.[66]

None of the regional governments have a strategy to sort, adjudicate, and manage the many thousands of men (and women) who are being held on suspicion of collusion with extremist groups. Currently, they are languishing in overflowing prisons, with little prospect of formal charges or trial. Among those captured are hardline ideologues and criminal opportunists, leaders and followers, adults and children. Many were forcibly conscripted, and others (including many girls and women) were kidnapped and subsequently indoctrinated. Ascribing culpability and providing a sense of justice for victims will be a long and difficult process.

The greatest uncertainty will be whether the current crisis prompts regional governments to undertake reforms that will address structural drivers of extremism and insecurity and ensures the integration of marginalized communities into the national economy and polity. There is little sign that Chadian President Deby, in power for 26 years, will loosen his repressive hold on power and move toward more inclusive governance. Neither is it likely that Cameroonian president Paul Biya, in office for 34 years, will leave without a political tussle.

In Mali, allegations of corruption and "business as usual" have seen President Ibrahim Boubacar Keita's popularity plummet since his election in September 2013. Niger's democracy remains fragile since a return to civilian rule in 2011. Despite Nigeria's democratic credentials, political intrigue and corruption continue to hamper inclusive development; progress there will depend on concerted effort at both the state and federal level.

Establishing mechanisms for participatory governance will require capable, empowered, and accountable local government institutions, which are often communities' only interface with the nation state. Delivery of public services, investment in agriculture and income-generating

---

[66] Interview with human rights defender Moussa Tchangari, in Niamey, January 19, 2016. A native of the Diffa region, Tchangari was imprisoned for 10 days after drawing attention to the plight of those displaced, accused of collusion with Boko Haram.

activities, and investment in infrastructure that connects domestic markets and reinforces national cohesion will be critically important.

Education—to provide life-skills, critical thinking, economic opportunity, and a sense of social cohesion—was most often cited as a priority for long-term investment. "Unless we invest massively in education," said Borno State Governor Kashim Shettima, "our security situation now is just an appetizer for future disaster."[67]

Regional Responses

Essential to preventing the regeneration of extremist alliances in the Sahel and Lake Chad Region will be cooperation among regional states to block supply routes, eradicate rear bases and training camps, share intelligence, and block the movement of fighters. Coordinating regional military efforts has been a halting process. Language barriers, competing regional membership groupings, different levels of threat perception, and distrust among the various state players have hampered effective joint action.

In the Lake Chad Basin, the regional Multinational Joint Task Force (MNJTF), comprising Benin, Cameroon, Chad, Niger, and Nigeria, has been slow to mobilize. The task force has struggled to meet its estimated $700 million budget as low global oil prices have squeezed government revenues in both Chad and Nigeria.

The relationship between Chad and Nigeria has been fraught with tension and mutual recriminations. As Boko Haram gained in strength and sophistication, Nigerian officials criticized the Chadian government's unwillingness to disrupt the flows of weaponry into North East Nigeria or take on Boko Haram's rear bases on Chadian territory. Chadian officials, for their part, have publicly rebuked Nigeria as "absent" in the fight against Boko Haram.[68] Some Nigerian security analysts accuse Chadian President Idriss Deby of political grandstanding. In 2014 Deby claimed to have won agreement from Boko Haram to join a cease-fire and enter a negotiation process. While the Nigerian military agreed to the cease-fire, the negotiations failed to materialize,[69] giving Boko Haram an opportunity to regroup and rearm.

In 2015 Deby's public claim that Shekau had been killed and that a new, previously unknown leader was ready to negotiate likewise proved false. Deby, for his part, claimed that Nigeria had sought the negotiations and cease-fire against his recommendation. Some media analysts suggest a more nefarious agenda: they point to the close personal relationship between Deby and former Borno State Governor Sheriff, an alleged sponsor of the group, who has significant business interests in Chad, including exploration licenses in the Chadian waters of Lake Chad.[70]

---

[67] Interview with Borno state governor Kashim Shettima in Maiduguri, January 11, 2016.

[68] Adam Nossiter, "Chad Strongman Says Nigeria Is Absent in Fight against Boko Haram," *New York Times*, March 27, 2015, http://www.nytimes.com/2015/03/28/world/africa/chad-strongman-says-nigeria-is-absent-in-fight-against-boko-haram.html?_r=0.

[69] "How Chadian President Fooled Nigeria on Phantom on Boko Haram Ceasefire," *The Cable*, November 9, 2014, https://www.thecable.ng/revealed-chadian-president-fooled-nigeria-phantom-boko-haram-ceasefire.

[70] CSIS interview with senior journalists in Abuja, January 10, 2016. See also "Chad 'Fuelling' Boko Haram Insurgency with Eyes on Borno Oil Deposits," *The Cable*, November 23, 2014, https://www.thecable.ng/exclusive-chad-fuelling-

Others dismiss these suspicions as conspiracy. The two countries have sparred over the headquarters and financing of the MNJTF as well.

Cooperation among members of the MNJTF has improved somewhat in 2016. The Nigerian military has announced joint patrols with Cameroon and conducted operations for which Chadian jets provided air cover.[71] Forces from Chad and Niger have worked well together, according to senior military officers in Niamey.

But as Boko Haram weakens, some worry that the commitment and cooperation of regional players will wane before the group is defeated entirely. Chadian officials already complain of being overstretched, with insecurity on all their borders—from Central African Republic to their south, Darfur to the west, Libya to the north, AQIM to the east, in addition to Lake Chad in their southwest corner. In Nigeria, Boko Haram is lower on the Buhari government's long list of priorities, as attacks by Fulani herdsmen on agricultural communities escalate,[72] and as militant groups in the Niger Delta degrade the country's crude oil production—the principal source of government revenue. Following through on progress made to date may prove increasingly difficult for the two most militarily capable members of the MNJTF.

In the Sahel, French and European support bolsters efforts by the G-5 Sahel, a regional group created in 2014 by the governments of Mali, Niger, Burkina Faso, Mauritania, and Chad. Member nations' militaries, with support from Opération Barkhane, have conducted coordinated operations along border areas. Regional forces are obliged to remain on their respective sides of the border since members have not yet come to agreement on mixed units, joint patrols, or the terms for hot pursuit.[73] "They have had a lot of meetings," said a skeptical Senegalese Air Force officer, "but they have accomplished very little. The G-5 is an empty drum."[74]

The African Union has pressed for a broader grouping, to include Senegal, Côte d'Ivoire, Guinea, and Algeria in addition to the G-5 members. Notably absent is Morocco—it is not a member of the Africa Union and has a long-standing feud with neighboring Algeria. Algeria, a critical player with unique military capabilities and intelligence on AQIM, has been loath to participate in multilateral efforts. In 2010, it established a joint military headquarters (CEMOC, the Comité d'état major opérationnel conjoint) to coordinate counterterror efforts with Mali, Mauritania, and Niger, but the grouping has had little impact. Military officials in Niger, however, describe a strong bilateral relationship with Algeria, which supports improved surveillance along the two countries' shared border, and works with the Nigerien military to disrupt the flow of fighters, traffickers, and migrants in Niger's far north.

---

boko-haram-insurgency-eyes-borno-oil-deposits; Eric Draitser, "Unraveling the Mystery of Boko Haram," *Counter Punch*, January 27, 2015, http://www.counterpunch.org/2015/01/27/unraveling-the-mystery-of-boko-haram/.
[71] Chris Stein, "Multinational Force Fighting Boko Haram Gets Mixed Results," VOA, July 15, 2016, http://www.voanews.com/a/multinational-force-fighting-boko-haram-gets-mixed-results/3420173.html.
[72] Institute for Economics and Peace, *Global Terrorism Index 2015*.
[73] Interview with African Union representatives in Bamako, October 7, 2015.
[74] Interview in Dakar with senior Senegalese military official, October 4, 2015.

International Efforts

The United States, along with the United Kingdom and European Union, has focused its efforts on training and partner capacity building, with Special Operations Forces playing a leading role. The United States has refrained from direct military interventions but provides support for intelligence collection and surveillance, with drones and fixed-wing aircraft operating out of bases in Niger and Burkina Faso.

France has taken the most prominent and direct role in battling violent extremism across the Sahel. Sahelian terror groups pose a more direct threat to French interests than they currently do to those of the United States or other European states. France maintains strong business and military links with its former Sahelian colonies, and thousands of French citizens still live in states across the Sahel and the West African region. AQIM's Algerian leadership considers France to be its primary enemy, and resentment against the French colonial occupation is long-standing and widespread in Algeria and the upper Sahel. France is also home to a large French-Algerian diaspora, elements of which helped fund AQIM's antecedent organizations and to whom AQIM leaders may still maintain links.

At the center for France's current engagement is Operation Barkhane, a 3,000-strong expeditionary force headquartered in N'Djamena, with bases in Burkina Faso, Niger, and Côte D'Ivoire. Its objective is to work with counterparts in Burkina Faso, Chad, Mauritania, and Niger to pursue, capture, and eliminate AQIM and its affiliates and prevent them from rebuilding camps and safe havens. It operates through small, highly mobile units across a broad territorial expanse. Barkhane's mandate expanded in 2015 to provide logistic and intelligence support to MNJTF countries in the fight against Boko Haram.

MINUSMA tasks include supporting the implementation of the peace agreement by the Malian government and armed groups, and helping extend state authority across the north. While its mandate is to take robust and active measures to protect civilians and UN personnel from asymmetrical attacks, its remit does not technically extend to violent extremist organizations.

On paper, MINUSMA and Barkhane are focused on two different sets of players—MINUSMA on armed groups and Barkhane on terrorists. In reality, they are often looking at the same individuals, but with different objectives—MINUSMA to engage, and Barkhane to neutralize. The lack of communication and intelligence sharing between the two operations is a source of frustration among some MINUSMA personnel.

04

Conclusion: Challenges for International Engagement

Extremist organizations comprise one among many sets of players contributing to insecurity in the Sahel. They operate to varying degrees in concert or in competition with criminal enterprises, ethnic militias, armed groups, and corrupt government authorities. All these various actors have a common interest in keeping the government in a weak position where it cannot—or will not—enforce the rule of law.

Moreover, any effort seeking to eliminate extremism without also tackling these other networks will ultimately fail. This will be particularly difficult in the Sahel, where all of the above actors overlap in complicated ways and where narcotics trafficking is such a lucrative and established industry. The landscape is somewhat less fragmented in the Lake Chad region, although there too, vested interests, corrupt local authorities, and a conflict economy will pose a continued challenge.

Four interrelated developments across the Sahel and Lake Chad region warrant close attention in the year ahead.

First, as regional extremist groups come under pressure, there is a strong possibility that they will seek to strengthen existing alliances as well as forge new ones. Particularly worrisome is the possibility that these groups will inspire and align themselves with other groups or leaders mobilized around perceived grievances, allowing them to tap into ready-made networks across an expanded geographic area.

Second, as military advances undermine organizations' image of invincibility, extremist leaders may seek to distinguish themselves from other groups through high-profile operations beyond the Sahel and Lake Chad Basin, where unfortunately, attacks on local populations have become almost too routine to garner global headlines. With territorial acquisition no longer an option, occasional but spectacular attacks in urban settings across West Africa will be the most viable and visible way for these groups to advertise their relevancy and capability.

A third development to watch will be the growing ties between local groups and global terror networks. Declaring their allegiance to al Qaeda and ISIL allowed AQIM and Boko Haram, respectively, to deflect attention from their relatively weak positions, burnish their organizational credentials, and increase their chances of receiving funding, training, and operational advice from the more established groups. Conversely, as al Qaeda and ISIL come under increasing international pressure, they too will have incentive to strengthen those vertical ties. The actions of local affiliates demonstrate their global reach, expand the pool of potential recruits, and can provide sanctuary for fighters fleeing Syria, Iraq, and Libya.

Finally, the political vacuum in Libya has drawn extremist fighters from across the Middle East. ISIL has gained a foothold (however tenuous) in the coastal area around Sirte, and al Qaeda is working through its local affiliate, Ansar al Sharia, in the eastern part of the country. Libya draws extremist fighters across the Sahel. But as Libyan and international forces press ISIL and al Qaeda strongholds, this flow could quickly reverse, sending fighters back into the Sahel, emboldened by new weaponry, experience, and new partners. "Boko Haram and AQIM are big problems for us," remarked a senior military intelligence officer in Niger, "but our biggest concern is what happens in Libya, because that could make things much, much more difficult. We have seen that already when Qaddafi fell. And our president is warning Western governments to think through the consequences this time."[75]

America's Stake

What should this mean to the United States? The United States, along with regional and international partners, cannot be complacent about extremism and insecurity in the Sahel. The lack of an immediate threat to the American homeland or to other critical interests does not mean one may someday emerge, nor that Boko Haram and AQIM can't destabilize important African partners and communities. The United States should support regional government efforts at preventing extremist groups from regrouping or expanding their geographical reach.

There is a demand for U.S. and partner support to regional security forces, helping them acquire the capacities and skills needed for an effective, calibrated response to extremist organizations. In that support, the United States must be insistent on making civilian protection a priority, with a strong emphasis on military ethics, accountability mechanisms, and institutional reform.

At the same time, the United States must be wary of privileging military assistance over other forms of engagement and reinforcing the tendency of regional governments to rely solely on military solutions. The United States ought to support strongly a much broader response from regional governments. Community policing is needed to ensure the security of citizens in remote and far-flung towns over the longer term and strengthening law enforcement should be an important priority.

Equally important is supporting efforts to sort and adjudicate the many thousands of people detained on suspicion of collaborating with extremist organizations, offer an off-ramp or reintegration process for ex-fighters where appropriate, and ensure that overcrowded and badly serviced prisons do not become an incubator for future extremists. These critical efforts must be pursued.

---

[75] Olivier Monnier, "Niger Says Conflict in Libya Biggest Threat to West Africa," Bloomberg, February 4, 2016, http://www.bloomberg.com/news/articles/2016-02-04/niger-says-conflict-in-libya-biggest-threat-to-west-africa.

The plight of the millions of civilians displaced by extremist violence, especially in the Lake Chad region, is of urgent concern. Millions of people in the region are at risk of starvation,[76] and hundreds have already died of hunger. U.S. interests align with those of regional governments insomuch as they seek stability, good governance, and respect for human rights. To this end, the United States ought to consider expanding existing development programs to address some of the immediate needs of these communities, including food aid and assistance for security services for IDP camps. Maintaining a hierarchy of priorities emphasizing and contributing to long-term, sustainable goals implemented by regional partners offers promise for future stability.

Finally, the United States should urge governments of the region to support marginalized communities, integrating them into the national economy. Focusing on strengthening the rule of law, while investing in security, education, and infrastructure, will allow for greater economic opportunity for these communities. Military interventions will remain a critical tool in these governments' strategies; but fundamental changes in governance are essential to erode the appeal and reemergence of violent extremist groups. This broader approach is long overdue—and is critical before greater threats reach in the Sahel.

---

[76] Ashish Kumar Sen, "Millions in Nigeria Are Starving, Warns UN Official," Atlantic Council, April 15, 2016, http://www.atlanticcouncil.org/blogs/new-atlanticist/millions-in-nigeria-are-starving-warns-un-official.

About the Authors

Jennifer G. Cooke is director of the CSIS Africa Program, where she manages a range of projects on political, economic, and security dynamics in Africa, providing research and analysis to U.S. policymakers, members of Congress, and the U.S. military, as well as the broader public. Cooke has authored and coauthored numerous CSIS reports, including *Rethinking Engagement in Fragile States* (2015), *Religious Authority and the State in Africa* (2015), *The State of African Resilience* (2015), and *Africa's New Energy Producers: Making the Most of Emerging Opportunities* (2015). She is a frequent commentator on Africa in print and electronic media and has testified before Congress on Boko Haram, the political crisis in Côte d'Ivoire, and the African Union. She holds an M.A. in African studies and international economics from the Johns Hopkins University School of Advanced International Studies (SAIS) and a B.A. in government, magna cum laude, from Harvard University. She has lived in Côte d'Ivoire and the Central African Republic.

Thomas M. Sanderson is director of the CSIS Transnational Threats Project, where he works on terrorism, transnational crime, global trends, and intelligence. He is currently investigating the "foreign fighter" phenomenon, as well as violent extremist activity across Africa. Sanderson has conducted field work in nearly 70 countries, where he has engaged militants, traffickers, intelligence officials, journalists, social activists, nongovernment organizations, and clergy. His articles have been published in the *New York Times* and *Washington Post*, and he is a consultant to the U.S. government and the private sector. Sanderson held fellowships in Berlin (2005) and in Shanghai (2001), and he earned a B.A. from Wheaton College (Massachusetts) and an M.A. from the Fletcher School at Tufts University.